12-STEP WORKBOOK FOR RECOVERING ALCOHOLICS, INCLUDING POWERFUL 4TH-STEP WORKSHEETS

2015 REVISED EDITION

IAM PASTAL

BALBOA.
PRESS
A DIVISION OF HAY HOUSE

Balboa Press books may be ordered through booksellers or by contacting:

Balboa Press
A Division of Hay House
1663 Liberty Drive
Bloomington, IN 47403
www.balboapress.com
1 (877) 407-4847

ISBN: 978-1-5043-2966-8 (sc)
ISBN: 978-1-5043-2967-5 (e)

Print information available on the last page.

Balboa Press rev. date: 08/07/2015

CONTENTS

FROM THE AUTHOR

By no means can this book be used to replace AA's Big Book, the "12 and 12" or any other aspect of AA. For me, and for many other AA members (who have used the worksheets), the 4th Step worksheets contained in this book have proved to be a valuable tool to accomplishing this inventory step. Additionally, the Step 7 approach described in this book provides you with a simple yet powerful way to use prayer with respect to your own individual character defects.

To the best of my knowledge, there is nothing in this book which contradicts anything contained in the AA literature.

Please note that where I have used individual names in this book, the names have been changed.

I would like to take this opportunity to thank AA (Bill, Bob and all who have followed) for:

1. All the wonderful relationships I have today with thousands of people,

2. My relationship with God, as I understand God,

3. All of the serenity and peace of mind I have today,

4. All material things in my life today, and

5. A life beyond all dreams.

A brief summary of my own story is that I grew up in a family of five children learning good discipline, morals and respect for others. After high school I pursued a professional career which allowed me to earn a large salary. At the age of 26 I married and my wife and I had two children - today, our daughter is 36 and our son is 34 and they are both friends of mine today.

My wife and I stayed married for 17 years. Following my marital break-up, my drinking increased significantly and naturally my job performance deteriorated significantly such that 2-½ years later my employer had no choice but to fire me - I had been with that company for nearly 20 years.

Shortly after our divorce in 1994, I married for the second time. This wife, however, was much smarter than my first wife. Whereas my first wife stayed with me for 17 years, this second wife left me about two months after we got married. (Please feel free to laugh with me on this.)

Following a very chaotic 2-year period, my life began to settle down in 1997 when I had my last drink as a direct result of the Fellowship and the 12-Steps of AA.

In 1998, a friend gave me a book entitled "A Course in Miracles" (ACIM) and, since 1999, I have been studying this book on a regular basis. The combined effect of AA and ACIM has enhanced my level of contentment and happiness more than words can express. Therefore, once you have ingrained the 12 steps into your life, I recommend you take a look at ACIM - to my knowledge, all major bookstores in the United States carry this book.

In 2006, I married for the 3rd time and my wife is an active member in Al Anon which I 100% endorse. In December of 2006 our first child was born stillborn which caused some real emotional upheaval in me but I never thought about drinking. In November of 2007 we were blessed with a healthy and happy baby girl who is now 7 and doing great. In late 2009, my wife gave birth to another little girl – unfortunately, her lungs never developed and she died in the hospital when she was about 2 months old. This loss, however, did not rock my emotions as did the loss of our first child. In March of last year (2014), our family was blessed with a perfectly healthy and happy baby boy (Iam Junior) who has added another level of happiness to our family life.

My life today is far better than I ever dreamed it could be - even as a child. This is directly attributable (1) to becoming a falling down drunk, (2) to being granted the gift of sobriety through AA, and (3) to an ever evolving spiritual life (I continue making spiritual progress).

My pen name, Iam Pastal, means to me that <u>I am past al</u>cohol. I'm quite convinced that I'll never drink again if I don't let up on my current way of life - I still attend about 10 AA meetings a week, I do a lot of service work (including sponsoring new members through the steps), try to maintain the unity of AA and practice the AA spiritual principles in all my affairs. I also spend some time each day studying A Course in Miracles.

P.S. If you believe you're an alcoholic, note that approximately 90% of alcoholics in the United States die miserable lonely deaths. The progression of the disease causes them to become ever more bitter and miserable over time. Therefore, I urge you to take the miraculous program of Alcoholics Anonymous very seriously because your life depends on it.

STEP 1

WE ADMITTED WE WERE POWERLESS OVER ALCOHOL - THAT OUR LIVES HAD BECOME UNMANAGEABLE

I break this step into 3 components:

(1) WE

I could not have done this "not drinking" life without you other members of AA.

(2) ADMITTED WE WERE POWERLESS OVER ALCOHOL

I can't drink safely.

(3) THAT OUR LIVES HAD BECOME UNMANAGEABLE

If you're having difficulty identifying with this part of Step 1, it is suggested you do a written review of past problems in your life and write down whether beer or booze was at the root of each problem. It is also important to know that alcoholism is a progressive disease. So if it appears to you that your life is still manageable because you can say "Nothing horrendous has happened to me", it's suggested you modify your statement slightly by saying "Nothing horrendous has happened to me <u>yet</u>."

Many people know they can't drink safely but continue drinking until they hit some deep pit in their life. While you are the only one who can decide, I would suggest to you that if you know you can't drink safely yet you continue to drink anyway, then you are in fact an alcoholic - you do not need to wait until your life becomes 100% unmanageable and totally miserable before you join the happy road to recovery, though sometimes difficult road in early recovery. In other words you can keep it real simple for yourself and shorten this Step 1 to "WE ADMITTED WE WERE POWERLESS OVER ALCOHOL."

STEP 2

CAME TO BELIEVE THAT A POWER GREATER THAN OURSELVES COULD RESTORE US TO SANITY

Sanity is a state of mind. Today, on those rare occasions when I think about drinking or drugging, I am insane. Although such insane thoughts can cross my mind, I have not come close to picking up a drink or a drug for many years.

My primary purpose today is to help new AA members achieve sobriety. History tells us that, prior to AA, the chance of someone with the disease of alcoholism ever recovering was extremely small. [This point is made in "THE DOCTOR'S OPINION" (pps. xxv-xxxii, 4th edition of AA's Big Book) and the experience of the famous psychiatrist, Dr. Carl Jung (pps. 26-27 of AA's Big Book).] However, in my 15 years as a sober member of AA, I have never seen an alcoholic not recover if he or she <u>thoroughly</u> follows AA's path.

I am convinced that God, by Himself, could not have helped me get sober. I clearly needed AA back in 1997 when I "Put the plug in the jug" and I love AA more today than I ever did. For these reasons, I emphasize that the physical earthly "Power Greater than Ourselves" in this Step 2 is Alcoholics Anonymous. Those in AA who continue to work the 12 steps discover a God Who is all understanding, all forgiving and all loving and not the punishing God defined in the religions of the Western World.

We in AA are a power much greater than me and so is God. The life I have today comes from both AA and God - I plan to stay with both for the rest of my earthly life.

If you do not believe in God, simply let AA be the "Power Greater Than Yourself". Additionally, a prayer along the following lines will help a lot: "God, if You are here, please relieve me of my drinking thoughts or at least keep me away from a drink today." At the end of the day, you should add something like: "God, whether you're here or not, thanks because I didn't drink today." "Fake it 'til you make it" is a great slogan as regards prayer for atheists and agnostics.

As indicated in our literature, the only people who seem to scoff at prayer are (1) those who haven't tried it enough and (2) those who dictate to God what they want from Him rather than ask Him what His Will is for them.

STEP 3

MADE A DECISION TO TURN OUR WILL AND OUR LIVES OVER TO THE CARE OF GOD AS WE UNDERSTOOD HIM

Here are two things AA says about God: (1) "He is the Father, and we are His children." (from page 62 of the Big Book); and (2) "We are sure God wants us to be happy, joyous, and free." (from page 133 of the Big Book). For the AA founders and for those of us who practice all 12 steps today, we are sure God wants this for all people.

In the 17 years I have followed the 12 steps of AA, my level of happiness has increased beyond measure and it continues to increase with time. This can happen for you, also, if you do the steps for yourself.

The phrase "happy, joyous and free" also means deeply contented or at peace. It is not disrupted by fear, anger, resentment, frustration, guilt and the like because, with God and AA's help, these feelings have been virtually eliminated from our being.

It may be impossible to be happy, joyous and free all the time while we are still in our bodies; it may be only achievable in the hereafter. However, I am living proof that it is possible to be in this condition over 97% of the time.

It is important to recognize that this feeling of being happy, joyous and free is all internal and that no one, in their right mind, would say they don't want this feeling. It is also a "now" condition and is not based on projections of future events. It, of course, includes the absence of guilt and fear. It allows one to function in this world without anger, impatience, intolerance, and stress while being honest and open-minded.

So many AA members (old and new) make such a big deal about this step. The truth is it is extremely simple - you do, in fact, want to be happy, joyous and free so make the decision. However, as noted in the Big Book, this decision has little effect unless you, at once, start on your written Step 4 inventory. After Step 4 there are of course 8 more steps to complete followed by a lifetime of action as we do our best to turn our will and lives over to the care of God as we understand Him.

As noted in the Big Book, the wording of the Step 3 prayer is optional. Following this paragraph is a modified 3rd step prayer which I recommend. One difference is that the Big Book prayer includes the request: "May I do Thy will always!" which is an impossible request - it is asking that we make no more mistakes and become perfect (i.e., that we become saints) which is not possible for a long time. (Remember, we claim spiritual progress, rather than spiritual perfection.) By contrast, the following prayer asks God that we do His Will better and better (that is, make 'spiritual progress') "One Day at a Time".

MODIFIED 3RD STEP PRAYER

Dear God,

I've made a mess of trying to manage my life. I have proved I can't do it. Also, I want to become happy, joyous and free which I understand You also want for me.

Therefore, I've made a decision to turn my will and my life over to You. Please relieve me of the prison of my selfish mind so I can better do Your Will. Please take away my difficulties, beginning with my disease of alcoholism, so that victory over them can demonstrate to others Your Power, Your Love and Your Way of Life. Please help me with my Step 4 written inventory.

May I do Your Will better and better "One Day at a Time".

Thank You God very much.

Now, we beg of you to move on to Step 4 "at once".

STEP 4

MADE A SEARCHING AND FEARLESS MORAL INVENTORY OF OURSELVES

Please don't let this title (searching, fearless, moral) scare you. This step is both interesting and beneficial beyond anything you can imagine. It's also very easy when the attached worksheets are used.

It's clear that God's Will (which is what you decided on in Step 3) is for you to proceed with Step 4 which not only looks at issues which block you from Him, but removes a lot of them too.

The attached Step 4 worksheets were taken from the instructions contained in Chapter 5 of the Big Book and from Step 4 of the "12 and 12". Following are some helpful comments:

1. All Step 4 requires is time and honesty.

2. Completing the worksheets requires uninterrupted quiet time - no phones or people should be disturbing you. Ask God for guidance on this. If you have a very busy schedule, a longer period on weekends may be better than trying to squeeze small amounts of time during the weekdays.

3. If you have a fear of doing Step 4, go first to the "FEARS" worksheet and put this fear down - when you get to the third column, sincerely ask God to remove this fear.

4. The first worksheet has you look into your resentments (1: RESENTMENTS). Columns 4 and 5 are prayers and will aid immensely in reducing or eliminating your resentments.

   If you have a resentment against yourself or against God, put these down. (By the way, both of these are quite common.)

   You will likely have more than 12 resentments - simply add extra pages as necessary. (This is true of all the worksheets.)

   You might really want to make some amends at this point - please don't. As a rule, you are not ready for this until you get to Step 9. Talk to your sponsor if you think otherwise.

5. Worksheet "2: FEARS" is real simple. The answer to the second question of Column 2 is usually 'yes', self-reliance failed me. In Step 3, however, we decided to rely on God rather than ourselves so the solution to any fear problem is contained in Column 3. Sometimes you'll get suggestions from your sponsor or others to do something to help overcome a fear. Since God works through people, seriously consider such input and pray with regard to it.

6. Regarding worksheet "3: HARMS TO OTHERS", both sexual and non-sexual harms should be included. If it's easier, you can have 2 separate worksheets for these 2 classifications.

   The Big Book suggests that we ask God what we should do about each specific harm; hence, the prayer included in column 3. In the majority of cases, amends for past harms will be done when you get to Step 9. In some cases, however, some earlier amends are important – for instance, if you are living or working with someone to whom you had caused serious harm. When considering any such preliminary amends, it is important that you discuss your intentions with an experienced AAer, usually your sponsor.

   If you carry guilt over something you did but where no one else was harmed, you have harmed yourself and any such activities should be included (here or as a resentment against yourself or as a fear that you might do it again).

7. Worksheet "4: SEX CONDUCT." Part [A] of this worksheet, where you are asked to list your uncomfortable sexual experiences, is recommended in the last paragraph on page 50 of the "12 and 12" which begins with "When, and how, and in just what instances, etc….?"

   Parts [B] and [C] will provide you with a plan for your future sex life, which, as far as you know, will be in accord with God's Will for you.

8. Two important final comments: (a) Don't even think about doing a perfect 4th step because there is no such thing; and (b) This Step 4 material forms the basis for your discussion with your Step 5 sponsor. If you plan to take something to the grave and never tell a soul, change this plan - it must be shared for your sake (in all likelihood, you will drink again if you don't share it with another person and, for an alcoholic, to drink is to die).

Please have fun looking at yourself!

Additional comment on resentments - These are things which "rent space in your head" so peace of mind is elusive at best. The most difficult ones are often found among persons closest to you. As a result of your past drinking, these people often have resentments against you too. It has been found that the best way for you to help such people is to "not drink" "One Day At A Time". Forgiveness (letting go of resentments) can, like recovery itself, take a long time for some of your resentments but God and AA are here to help you if you try.

1: RESENTMENTS

Column 1	Column 2	Column 3	Column 4	Column 5
I am resentful at – With 'who or what' am I angry?	The cause or causes – Why am I angry?	Disregarding the faults of the 'who or what', where was I to blame?	Pray: "Dear God, Save me from being angry, and/ or How do I forgive the 'who or what'?"	Pray for the 'who or what'; e.g., "Dear God, Please let Sam have peace of mind, health and happiness like I want for myself."

Columns 4 and 5 – "We asked God to help us show them the same tolerance, pity. and patience that we would cheerfully grant a sick friend. When a person offended we said to ourselves, 'This is a sick man. How can I be helpful to him? God save me from being angry. Thy will be done'" (page 67 of Big Book)

2: FEARS

Column 1	Column 2	Column 3
Who or what do I fear?	Why do I have this fear? Is it because self-reliance failed me?	Pray: "Dear God, please remove this fear or direct my attention to what else I need do to overcome this fear?"

3: HARMS TO OTHERS

Column 1	Column 2	Column 3
Who did I hurt?	Where was I at fault? What should I have done instead?	Pray: "Dear God, what should I do about this specific matter?"

4: SEX CONDUCT

[A]

First, look at your past uncomfortable sex experiences. These can be considered your past mistakes. We want to avoid these in the future. As stated on page 69 of our Big Book: "In this way we tried to shape a sane and sound ideal for our future sex life."

Now, go back through your life and describe your uncomfortable sexual experiences:

_____

_____

_____

_____

_____

_____

_____

_____

_____

_____

_____

_____

[B]

Now, using common sense, including a desire not to harm yourself or anyone else, asking God for help, set down your plan for your future sex life:*

_____

_____

[C]

Thinking about your plan (from [B], above), ask: "Dear God, is my plan okay?" If not, modify it accordingly:*

_____

_____

* "We asked God to mold our ideals and help us to live up to them." - page 69 of our Big Book.

STEP 5

ADMITTED TO GOD, TO OURSELVES, AND TO ANOTHER HUMAN BEING THE EXACT NATURE OF OUR WRONGS

Step 4 was the big mountain you had to climb. If you were honest with looking at yourself and sincerely asked God for help on each resentment and fear, you have come a long way in your spiritual growth.

I suggest Step 5 be a simple uninterrupted meeting with another person, usually your sponsor, where you review your Step 4 Worksheets. By this time, your sponsor probably knows a lot about you and can point out areas you may have missed or misled yourself.

If you don't trust your sponsor, you should get a new sponsor as soon as possible and do your 5th Step with your new sponsor.

It is possible there are certain aspects of your life you don't want to share with anyone; understand, however, that if you don't share these with someone you will, in all likelihood, drink again. The solution is simple - keep these parts separate from what you review with your sponsor but make an appointment with a religious leader to review this material with - for example, a priest, rabbi or minister. If you can find a religious leader who is also a recovering alcoholic, all the better.

Following your meeting with your sponsor (and, if applicable, religious leader), spend at least an hour in quiet and consider the first 5 steps to see if there is anything you might have missed; and thank God from the bottom of your heart that you know Him better (see page 75 of the Big Book).

STEP 6

WERE ENTIRELY READY TO HAVE GOD REMOVE ALL THESE DEFECTS OF CHARACTER

Steps 6 and 7 are sometimes referred to as the forgotten steps. If you see someone in AA who has some "sober" time in AA and is still angry and has the "life is a burden" attitude, he or she has never done these steps properly. These are the steps where the real miracles occur because we literally change at spiritual, mental and physical levels. What makes these Steps so simple is that we don't do it - God does it for us if we simply ask Him.

"We are sure God wants us to be happy, joyous, and free." (p. 133 of the Big Book) I agree with this statement 100% as I've come to understand God better and better through the teachings and the Fellowship of AA. The best definition of God I heard at an AA meeting - God is all forgiving, all understanding and all loving.

As I understand God today, God never punishes anyone. My own experience shows me that my many past pains and disturbances (to myself and others) always occurred when I was outside of God's Will. As I've made spiritual progress through AA, such 'bad' things are now reduced to "once in a while" events and I've become happier beyond any dreams I ever had.

Character defects effectively block our spirit from reaching God's Spirit. Step 6 should be automatic for the following reason - only God knows what will make me or you happy, joyous and free and, as our character defects are removed or reduced, we get closer to God; thus, if becoming happy, joyous and free is your

16

goal (and nobody with any sense would say otherwise), you must be ready to ask God to remove your defects.

If you have done a good job on Steps 4 and 5, it is fairly easy to know your specific character defects. The following Worksheet "5. CHARACTER DEFECTS OR SHORTCOMINGS" includes 20 human defects. (A brief definition of some of these defects is contained in Step 7 – see pages 20 and 21.) If you think you have others that don't fit any of the 20 listed, simply add them to this worksheet. Once you've completed this worksheet, which should only take a few minutes, review it with your sponsor.

5. CHARACTER DEFECTS OR SHORTCOMINGS

Column 1	Column 2
Defect	Rate this defect from 1 to 10, 10 being the worst.
Pride	
Lust	
Anger	
Greed	
Gluttony	
Envy	
Sloth	
Dishonest	
Selfish	
Self-Seeking Motives	
Low Self-Esteem (Reverse Pride)	
Inconsiderate	
Jealousy	
Bad Gossip	
Judgmental	
Resentment	
Controlling Others	
Folly	
People Pleasing	
Sarcasm	

STEP 7

HUMBLY ASKED HIM TO REMOVE OUR SHORTCOMINGS

With regard to Step 7, I suggest you look at your 20 defects (on page 17) and, where you see a need, ask God for their removal. When I sponsor someone, my rule is that if we have given them a rating of 5 or higher on a character defect then they will ask God to remove that defect as described below. If the rating is 4 or lower then they don't really have the defect but have an asset which is the opposite of the defect. For example, if their dishonest rating is 3, then they are essentially an honest person though they may occasionally be dishonest.

For most alcoholics, anger is one of the number one reasons we could drink again so I definitely recommend you ask God for the removal of this defect even if the rating is less than 5. What really helped me with my anger defect was simply but sincerely asking: "God, please remove my anger character defect."

This simple prayer request, when I was 10 months sober, was the first part of a major spiritual experience for me in my road to recovery. Before I asked God to do this for me, I was in the habit of verbally blowing up in anger (rage) 4 or 5 times a week when people weren't doing "what they were supposed to". One night, when I was 10 months sober, I got real angry at my girl friend's 12-year old son. The next day I sincerely asked God: "Please remove my anger defect." Although I asked Him to do this, I had no faith that it would work and so I didn't think about it for a while. About 6 weeks later I had this sudden realization that I hadn't blown up in anger since I asked God to remove this human defect from me - I was amazed! This was a powerful spiritual experience! God did for me what I couldn't do for myself - He changed me to become a much more loveable person with one small prayer. The truth is that I can still get angry, annoyed, intolerant, etc., from time to time but as I make spiritual progress, these flaws get reduced.

So for everyone doing Step 7, I suggest you ask "God, please remove my anger character defect."

If you can't seem to get rid of your resentments (i.e., your resentment defect is 5 or higher), go back to your "RESENTMENTS" worksheet and do it again. Then, sincerely ask: "God, please remove my resentment character defect."

With respect to the 20 defects listed in Worksheet 5 where your rating is 5 or higher, the prayers are as follows:

If you think you're better than others, ask "God, please remove my pride character defect."

If sex is a problem, ask "God, please remove my lust character defect."

Whether or not you think anger is a problem for you, ask "God, please remove my anger character defect."

If greed is a problem, ask "God, please remove my greed character defect."

If over eating is a problem, ask "God, please remove my gluttony character defect."

If you think you'd be happier if you had what others have, ask "God, please remove my envy character defect."

If you think you are lazy, ask "God, please remove my sloth character defect."

If being honest is a problem, ask "God, please remove my dishonest character defect."

If you seem to be always looking for 'what you can get' and seldom 'for what you can give', ask "God, please remove my selfish character defect".

If you often have self-seeking motives underlying your actions (e.g., I'll invite him to my party so I'll get invited to his), ask "God, please remove my self-seeking motives character defect."

If you think you are less than others, ask "God, please remove my low self-esteem character defect."

If you tend to be inconsiderate to others, ask "God, please remove my inconsiderate character defect."

If you find yourself upset or angered when someone shows affection or attention to a loved one (e.g., spouse, children), ask "God, please remove my jealousy character defect."

If you have a tendency to point negative fingers at others behind their back, ask "God, please remove my bad gossip character defect."

Judging others is internal bad gossip, even if you don't communicate it to others. If you have a tendency to find fault with other people, ask "God, please remove my judgmental character defect."

If you find some resentments continue such that you can't forgive a person (perhaps yourself) or situation, ask "God, please remove my resentment character defect."

If you feel compelled to try to control the lives of other people (e.g., parents who try and do this with their grown children), ask "God, please remove my controlling others character defect."

If you have a tendency to be a clown when others are serious, ask "God, please remove my folly character defect."

If you have an unhealthy need to be liked by others, ask "God, please remove my people pleasing character defect."

If you have a sarcastic tongue and attitude, ask "God, please remove my sarcasm character defect."

It is important, in my experience, to ask God specifically on each relevant defect even though you may have little or no faith He can change you at these levels - I know He can because He has done it for me.

A word of caution concerning 'sloth' - It seems to me that our Western culture has evolved to a point where persons are addicted to action. Even vacations seem to be filled with chaotic days where many people need time off after a vacation to recover from the hectic vacation days. Therefore, in considering this particular defect, with prayer, determine if you need to be less active, rather than more active. In this regard, note that God has a much easier time reaching a quiet mind.

Please note that, as a human being, I still have all of these defects but at a fraction of what they used to be. As indicated on page 65 of AA's 12 and 12, the removal of character defects is a "lifetime job". As I make "spiritual progress" in sobriety, these defects get reduced and I become more happy, joyous and free on an increasing basis.

On page 62 of the Big Book, the relationship between God and all people is defined as: "He is the Father, and we are His children." God is Spirit and we were all created in His likeness - in truth therefore, we are all spirit. In human form, our spirits are contaminated at different levels with the character defects discussed in this chapter. However, this contamination (or sickness) will disappear when we get to the hereafter where only truth will exist forever. Understanding this allows me to define ultimate humility very simply - God created each and every one of us and is above all of us; in truth, or in spirit, we are all equal.

STEP 8

MADE A LIST OF ALL PERSONS WE HAD HARMED, AND BECAME WILLING TO MAKE AMENDS TO THEM ALL

The list of people we had harmed was initially done on Worksheet 3 in Step 4. In this Step 8, however, consider whether any additional persons should be added.

The second part of this step is to be "willing to make amends to them all". Some might ask "Why should I be willing to do this?" The logical answer is that once Steps 8 and 9 are complete, you will be able to walk the planet a free person, not fearing who you might run into - the "wreckage of your past" will be cleaned up. It is really a wonderful feeling!

"Willingness" is the key here. In any amends situation, your plan must be to "never" point the finger at the person you will be making the amends to for, if you do, the relationship could end up worse after the "amends" than before. Your active role, when you do make amends, will be to (1) admit the harms you did (never mentioning any harms the other person may have done), (2) "clean up your side of the street" only which sometimes requires financial restitution, (3) possibly ask or suggest – never demand - the person forgive you (in whatever words work for you), and (4) "accept" the other persons reaction good or bad ("Let the chips fall where they will").

In considering your willingness, although you need not feel 100% confident when approaching the person you owe an amends to, it is important that you carry no significant resentment against the person. If you do, then you are not yet ready to make a person to person amends. In some of these cases, a carefully written amends letter should be considered (talk to your sponsor on this). Additionally, it is strongly suggested that you continue to use the prayer tools offered in the previous steps - for example, from column (4) of Worksheet 1, ask God how you can forgive this person and from Step 7, ask God to remove your anger and resentment character defects with respect to the individual you harmed. Do these prayers sincerely every day for a while and you will likely get positive results.

STEP 9

MADE DIRECT AMENDS TO SUCH PEOPLE WHEREVER POSSIBLE, EXCEPT WHEN TO DO SO WOULD INJURE THEM OR OTHERS

As noted in Step 8, when this step is complete you will be able to walk the planet a free person, not fearing anyone you might encounter - you will have cleaned up "the wreckage of your past".

It is important that you understand you are doing this step for yourself, not for the person you are making the amends to. In the majority of situations, however, the other person will be helped also.

Although this point was made in Step 8, it is so important that it is repeated here - in any amends situation, you must never point your finger at the person you're making amends to for, if you do, the relationship could end up worse after the "amends" than before. Your job is simply to admit your wrongs, "clean up your side of the street", possibly ask for forgiveness* and let the chips fall where they will. Even if the person doesn't accept your amends, you will feel a whole lot better if you do a good job.

In addition to the use of prayer before taking any action here, it is strongly suggested that you discuss each amends action with your sponsor.

Also consider carefully those to whom amends should not be made because it would injure them or other people. Two examples to help explain this thought are:

---

* When sincere, here is a very good forgiveness request which makes no demands on the other person: "I hope you can forgive me at some point for what I did."

(1) You had hurt an ex-lover but no longer see this person - to make amends to such a person could resurrect old hurts or feelings and could severely affect any new relationship that person is in. As a general rule, you should not make amends to such an individual.

(2) You have had one or more extra-marital affairs. If your spouse is unaware, it may be best not to divulge the information because of the harm to her or him. If your spouse is aware of your infidelity, then amends to her or him would, as a rule, be required; however, your spouse need not know who the third party is since this could cause harm to that third party.

Common sense suggests that if you owe someone money, do not make amends until you have the money owed or at least part of the money and a definite plan to pay off the balance.

There may be persons who are on your list but who are no longer a part of your life. The important thing is you're ready and willing to make amends with respect to such individuals - if God moves you to reach out and contact such persons, then by all means do so.

You will know when Step 9 is essentially complete when you are not concerned with who you might encounter no matter where you go.

STEP 10

CONTINUED TO TAKE PERSONAL INVENTORY AND WHEN WE WERE WRONG PROMPTLY ADMITTED IT

Steps 10, 11 and 12 effectively incorporate the first 9 steps and are often referred to as the maintenance steps.

In early sobriety, I often used what I refer to as the "PLAGGES" tool - PLAGGES is an acronym for the 7 defects (or plagues) of Pride, Lust, Anger, Greed, Gluttony, Envy and Sloth. Later on, I realized this list did not include one of the most important defects - Dishonesty. Today, I suggest the acronym D PLAGGES to remember these 8 major defects. With this tool, you can easily do a spot check inventory in your head when you're stopped at a light, going to the bathroom, having a meal, etc. For example, you can ask yourself, so far today have I been dishonest, prideful, lustful, angry, greedy, gluttonous, envious or slothful? Do I owe anyone an apology for anything I've done today?

In Step 10 of the 12 and 12 (page 90), it states "It is a spiritual axiom that every time we are disturbed, no matter what the cause, there is something wrong with us." I believe peace of mind is God's greatest gift to us and anger is perhaps the greatest threat to this gift. It is also the emotion which causes us to relapse more than any other. Today, whenever I get angry, I examine myself, and determine what I could have done instead - I learn from such experiences. Anger always separates but, with the help of the 12 steps, it can usually be corrected easily. From God's eyes, we are all His children and He wants us all to get along so His Will is for us is to become less and less angry and more at peace with ourselves and with others.

27

It is important that we discuss our anger with our sponsors, with others in AA with good sobriety, and, if necessary, at AA meetings. This lets persons with solutions know we have a problem. Others can then help us with this very challenging emotion. (A common mistake for many people is to share their angry feelings with friends who simply agree with them and might even offer suggestions for revenge. Revenge is never a good solution.)

It is important that a new person not be accumulating new resentments in early sobriety - otherwise, the new person may see 'sobriety' as more painful than the old drinking life and might 'go back out'. If, when sponsoring a new guy, I see him moving in this direction, I often review with him Step 10 from the '12 and 12' before he has completed the first 9 steps - the material in this chapter offers a host of powerful tools for handling the ups and downs of the day without getting 'bent out of shape' too much.

STEP 11

SOUGHT THROUGH PRAYER AND MEDITATION TO IMPROVE OUR CONSCIOUS CONTACT WITH GOD AS WE UNDERSTOOD HIM, PRAYING ONLY FOR KNOWLEDGE OF HIS WILL FOR US AND THE POWER TO CARRY THAT OUT

In Step 11 of the '12 and 12', in addition to prayer and meditation, self-examination is a part of our spiritual growth. As noted on page 98, when these three aspects "are logically related and interwoven, the result is an unshakable foundation for life".

For life to get better and better, as it has for me, you must be willing to grow spiritually and get and then improve your conscious contact with God. Conscious means you will feel His presence and hear His Will for you in words or thoughts through meditation (i.e., listening to God). A very good prayer to Him, which can be asked at any time, is: "What should I think or say or do, if anything?"

One of the best suggestions in the Big Book is that "on awakening, we think about the twenty-four hours ahead" and we pray. (p. 86) I have found if I don't let God in early in the day, I'm setting myself up for a bad day. On p. 87 of the Big Book, it is further suggested you ask God for help during the day - "As we go through the day, we pause, when agitated or doubtful, and ask for the right thought or action." I've found that telling God thank you or simply loving Him during the better parts of my day is also very helpful to me - an ungrateful individual can't understand what good sobriety means.

I believe the best measure as to whether you're making spiritual progress is whether you are more at peace and more happy than you were a week or a month ago. If the answer is no, I suggest you get some help from your sponsor or others because you're moving in the direction of a drink.

STEP 12

HAVING HAD A SPIRITUAL AWAKENING AS THE RESULT OF THESE STEPS, WE TRIED TO CARRY THIS MESSAGE TO ALCOHOLICS, AND TO PRACTICE THESE PRINCIPLES IN ALL OUR AFFAIRS

The first direction given in Step 12 is that we try to carry the AA recovery message to other alcoholics. Every alcoholic at an AA meeting, whether 1 day or 50 years without a drink, is carrying the message at some level. For those who have completed the first 11 steps, the direction given here is to sponsor newcomers - Chapter 7 of the Big Book (starting on page 89) covers this in excellent detail (although it doesn't use the words 'sponsor' or 'sponsee' because these terms had not yet evolved).

A good sponsor is extremely important to newcomers. For those of us who do sponsor newcomers, it is a privilege and a tremendous satisfaction. I can certainly identify with the following statement contained on page 110 of the "12 and 12" - "Practically every AA member declares that no satisfaction has been deeper and no joy greater than in a Twelfth Step job well done."

There are some AA members, though qualified, who don't sponsor newcomers. I see two major reasons for this, both based on unfounded fears. The first is they don't feel qualified. Well, if a person has in fact completed the first 11 Steps he or she is, by definition, qualified.

To these persons, please note that the written teaching tools for guiding a sponsee through the steps are contained in the Big Book, the "12 and 12", and, if you want, the tools contained in this book or others that can help to simplify certain aspects of the Steps. Your own experiences in recovery are really the only other thing you need - try it and, keep in mind, you've got God and, hopefully, your own good sponsor who can help you if you start getting too tangled up with a sponsee.

The second reason or fear is that they think their sponsee might relapse 'because of them'. They simply need to realize that they are not that powerful. Most newcomers will relapse - it's a fact. My own experience is that, even where a sponsee has relapsed, I have benefited tremendously while I was working with him (and those benefits are still with me today) - it's helped me and I know I've planted some recovery seeds in him which hopefully will help him to get sober some day.

So, if you're not sponsoring someone and have completed the first 11 steps (including a written 4th Step), hop on the happy, joyous and free bandwagon and ask God to put someone in your life to sponsor. [If you have not done a written 4th Step but have been sponsoring others (or claiming to), please stop - you can't sponsor anyone through Steps 4, 5, 6, 7, 8, 9, 10, 11 and 12 if you've never done a 4th Step which requires a written inventory.]

The second direction of Step 12 is that we practice these principles in all our affairs. For me, this has become very simple - the "We" of AA has been expanded to include all people on the planet for "We" are all God's children. I am learning how to forgive even the nastiest people I encounter. When I hit bumps in my road, through good sponsorship, self-examination, prayer and meditation I have been able to determine what I did wrong so I can hopefully do better next time.

I hope that you, like me, can really start identifying with: "The joy of living is the theme of A.A.'s Twelfth Step." (page 106 of the "12 and 12")

APPENDIX I
USEFUL PRAYERS

<u>Recovering Alcoholic's Morning Prayer:</u>

"God, please keep me away from a drink today."

<u>PPP - Powerful Peace Prayer:</u>

"God grant me peace, God grant me peace, etc., etc."…repeat mentally as often as necessary until you have the necessary peace.

APPENDIX II
DISCUSSION OUTLINE FOR AL (NOT HIS REAL NAME), A SPONSEE WHO RELAPSED

Your Mom - You can't change her. Accept that she will probably try and control your life and forgive her for this. God will help you if you ask Him.

Your girl friend (in AA) - Though she has some years under her belt, she appears to share at every meeting that her emotional sobriety stinks. Perhaps this is because she's been in sick (sex) relationships since early sobriety? It seems clear to me she's done no Steps 6 and 7 work with respect to 'lust' and 'dishonesty' defects; perhaps she's done no Step 7 work?

Ask God for help on all things. In particular, ask Him for help to change your thinking that the AA 'rooms' are a place to pick up women. You simply tell those that approach you "I'm here to get sober, not to get into a sex relationship!"

Your Mom, Dad and you - I laugh at this - It seems to me that all 3 of you know that you relapsed but you all lie about it to each other because honest heartfelt communication, so it is thought, would be difficult.

Al - Though you have grown spiritually, here's what you learned from your relapse:

1. You hadn't grown very much spiritually because you did what you and God knew was the worst thing you could ever do - you drank.

2. You learned at a deeper level what "cunning, baffling and powerful" means.

3. You learned the destructive power of "anger" as a trigger.

P.S. I learned these things too.

Our sobriety is dependent on our relationship with God, not people, places and things.

This relationship with God takes time - meetings, steps, giving back (Step 12), prayer, meditation, self-examination, etc. If this process moves forward for you, as it has for me, you will stop "reacting" to life based on Al's will but will let God give you directions because He knows what's best for you.

At your age, you should ask God for help in adopting the "self supporting" tradition into your life and get out from under your Mom and Dad's roof. As I've mentioned, a half way house is something I think you should look into.

As stated on page 120 of the Big Book regarding relapse, "You must redouble your spiritual activities if you expect to survive." I certainly don't see you doing this. I don't recall what grades you gave yourself on Worksheet 5, but now that I know you better, I see your lust defect up at the ten level, your anger/resentment defects are way up there, your dishonest defect is at the ten level and your greed defect is at the ten level.

On greed, first note a distinction between pleasure and happiness as follows - Good sex is pleasurable; a good steak is more pleasurable than a burnt hot dog; the smell of roses is more pleasurable than the smell of dog shit. Pleasure is defined by our five senses. Happiness, as I define it here, is a spiritual condition. Especially in early sobriety, I was much happier being around recovering alcoholics than I was being around my blood relatives. It is my opinion that you think happiness can be found in the pleasures of the world; in particular the nice house your parents continue to allow you to stay at. I say this because the times I've talked to you about getting an inexpensive place of your own or going to a halfway house, the suggestion fell on deaf ears. A nice apartment with a balcony where you could indulge in a nice cigar by yourself was your idea of your first step outside your parent's house.

During the few months you were working the steps with me, you were getting (spiritually) happy. In my opinion, this ended when you got into a pleasurable sexual relationship - your girl friend "goddess" got in between you and God, as you were beginning to understand Him.

Remember those happy months when you were growing spiritually - you can regain them and keep getting happier if you continue making spiritual progress.

You're back at the first word in Step 1 - "We" - AA's Fellowship. Had you understood this word, you would never have relapsed - you would have called another recovering person first. In this regard, you should call a different AA guy every night for the next 31 days simply saying you were told to do this by your sponsor if the guy needs to know. Also, ask the guy what meetings he regularly attends and perhaps he could take you to some. This should be your ride of first resort. If you start learning what the word "We" means, you should never need a ride to a meeting from your parents within a week from today.

"We claim spiritual progress...." As I've made spiritual progress the past 6+ years with AA as my foundation, I've gotten more and more happy. Also, the thought of a drink or a drug keeps moving further away. I also know that I can't stay sober today on what I did yesterday or in the past, no matter how hard "I" think "I" worked.

Please forgive me for suggesting to you that a sex relationship was okay for you at the time you jumped into it. To a very large extent, you immediately substituted "Al and her" for the little you knew of the power of "We". Also, I now realize Step 12 is definitely an 'action' step - simply because you and I had reviewed it didn't mean you had done anything about it. As defined by the 'Working With Others' chapter in the Big Book, a major part of Step 12 is working with a new guy and helping him get through the 12 steps for himself. (As a result of this mistake I made with you, I'll be telling new single sponsees they should not get into a relationship for at least a year or, if later, after initially doing all 12 steps including sponsoring a new guy through the steps.)

May God bless you as He has me.

Your sponsor and friend,
Iam Pastal

The 'Truth' Al - God is Love; He created us like Him so we are Love; We are all joined with each other and joined with God, our Creator forever.

APPENDIX III
STEP 3 DISCUSSION OUTLINE FOR CHARLIE (NOT HIS REAL NAME), A SPONSEE

Notes for Charlie - Step 3:

1. What this step means to you now – "I've made a decision to turn my will (and therefore my life) over to God, as I understand God."

2. Charlie - This is only a bare start on A.A.'s program. It is only a decision - you can decide to build a house but the decision, by itself, does not accomplish the job. At Step 3, you are a far cry from permanent sobriety and a contented, useful life. That's where the remaining steps (4 through 12), continued attendance at meetings, and fellowship with other AA winners comes in.

3. A spiritual life is not a theory even though it can't be proved scientifically – by definition, spirit is not within the physical realm. Normal people do not live a spiritual life so don't ever expect to be "normal". [Normal people also don't destroy their lives with alcohol and drugs - you don't have to live that way anymore.]

4. You can believe what I now know to be true as did the authors of the Big Book – God wants you to be happy, joyous and free (from within). This inward condition of happiness will get better and better if you progress spiritually in time. I really like this 6 word definition of the true God which I picked up at an AA meeting - He is "all loving, all forgiving, all understanding".

5. Referring to your 3rd Step decision and prayer, here's what the Big Book says at the top of page 64 "Though our decision was a vital and crucial step, it could have little permanent effect unless at once followed by a strenuous effort to face, and to be rid of, the things in ourselves which had been blocking us." (emphasis added) That is, the Step 4 written inventory should be done now.

6. So move on to Step 4 which you've already started, having listed your resentments, fears and harms.

APPENDIX IV
ON FORGIVING ONE'S SELF - LETTER TO AN AA FRIEND WITH 4 YEARS AWAY FROM A DRINK

[Author's note: Though it may appear otherwise, it is not my intention to endorse any religion in this letter. It has been my experience that religion and spirituality have nothing to do with each other. AA is a spiritual program. Personally, I belong to no religious organization.]

Dear Joe,

I hope you're feeling and doing good. I expect you've been busy getting ready for your move up north.

As we've discussed, you have a low self-esteem issue (or reverse pride per our AA literature). How does this get resolved? - By asking God.

The greatest teacher was Jesus - He's still with us (in Spirit, where it counts). Jesus kept it real simple and boiled life down to 2 simple suggestions: (1) Love God, and (2) Love your neighbor as you love yourself.

My own experience as I've sought God is that as I get to know God better I love myself better - God's forgiven me for all my past misdeeds here in the world and I know He's forgiven you too (but me knowing it doesn't help you - you have to know it). As I love myself better, I can love others better.

So how do you get rid of your low self-esteem? You simply ask God and then meditate (stop the committees in your head and let God in).

I'm not God but your prayer/meditation might go as follows:

Joe - Dear God, how can I forgive myself?

God - (pause for you to be still) - I'm smiling child (pause for Joe to feel Love) - You are forgiven.

Joe - How can you say that considering what I've done?

God - I am Love, I am Spirit, and I am eternal; and I created you like Me so you are love, you are spirit and you are eternal. The world does not know me but you are learning of me through the fellowship and the lessons in AA as well as the teachings of your elder brother, Jesus. The "truth" is that everyone in the world is forgiven for their misdeeds, no matter how evil they're perceived and everyone will come Home to Me in Heaven. You are my child and you are forgiven.

Of course, Joe, I don't know how God will communicate this truth to you. My suggestion, as a good friend, is to go somewhere for at least 1/2 hour where you can have peace and quiet - w/o your cell phone and ask God "How can I forgive myself?"

I'm really looking forward to spending time with you and Alice up north later this year. Meanwhile, we'll be in touch...Thanks for your help my friend....Iam.

Printed in the United States
By Bookmasters